W9-AAE-563

SEARCHING FOR

THE LOCH NESS MONSTER

rosen publishing's
rosen central

New York

Nikki Case
and Martin Delrio

Published in 2012 by The Rosen Publishing Group, Inc.
29 East 21st Street, New York, NY 10010

First Edition

Library of Congress Cataloging-in-Publication Data

Case, Nikki.
Searching for the Loch Ness monster/Nikki Case, Martin Delrio.
   p. cm.—(Mystery explorers)
Includes bibliographical references and index.
ISBN 978-1-4488-4763-1 (lib. bdg. : alk. paper)—
ISBN 978-1-4488-4772-3 (pbk. : alk. paper)—
ISBN 978-1-4488-4780-8 (6-pack : alk. paper)
1. Loch Ness monster—Juvenile literature. I. Delrio, Martin. II. Title.
QL89.2.L6C37 2011
001.944—dc22

2011008277

Manufactured in the United States of America

CPSIA Compliance Information: Batch #S11YA: For further information, contact Rosen Publishing, New York, New York, at 1-800-237-9932.

CONTENTS

INTRODUCTION

"**N**atural philosophy is now one of the favourite studies of the Scottish nation and Loch Ness well deserves to be diligently studied."

This was written by writer Dr. Samuel Johnson in 1773. For centuries, the legend of the Loch Ness monster has intrigued people from all economic groups, cultures, and races. It has been a fixture in popular culture ranging from literature, music, movies, comics, television shows, and even anime.

The legend of the Loch Ness monster began in one of the most intriguing places. It all started in Loch Ness, the deepest in Great Britain. Cut in the fault of Great Glen, which dissects the mountainous Highlands in the north of Scotland, Loch Ness is a popular tourist destination

Loch Ness is 24 miles (38.6 kilometers) long yet only about 1 mile (1.6 km) wide. Its maximum depth is 754 feet (230 meters). Because of its size, the loch, or lake, is nearly impossible to thoroughly search for unusual life-forms, which adds to the intrigue and mystery of the tale. To date, only about 60 percent of the lake has been scanned by sonar. Further adding to the difficulty of a search is that the lake has steep stone sides and varying temperatures, which make it difficult for a sonar to get accurate readings. These factors on top of the fact that other objects such as driftwood exist in the lake make it nearly impossible to find. Even the way the lake reflects light has added to the mystery and intrigue.

The reasons for the enduring popularity of the Loch Ness monster are vast. While there have been claimed sightings and photographs taken of the

In February 2011, two kayakers photographed on a cell phone camera "Bownessie," a Loch Ness-like creature inhabiting Windermere Lake in England, roughly 300 miles (482 km) away from Loch Ness.

supposed creature, there's still no scientific evidence of its existence. Ironically, this lack of proof may be the strongest reason why the legend is kept alive in the public consciousness. The curiosity about the creature keeps us coming back to the legend.

Other reasons might include our need for a mysterious and mythical figure in general. All societies have their version of the Loch Ness monster, whether it be American claims of UFO sightings in Roswell, New Mexico, or the Abominable Snowman sightings in the Himalayas. These mythical creatures give people a natural curiosity to thirst for and subsequently quench in the attempts to solve these mysteries.

In February 2011, there were claims to another sighting, this time in Lake Windermere, about 300 miles (482 km) from Loch Ness. The monster, nick-named "Bownessie," appeared to be about 50 feet (15.24 m) long. Kayakers Tom Pickles and Sarah Harrington managed to take a photograph of the beast. Pickles said, "Its skin was like a seal's, but its shape was completely abnormal." Gliding through the water at about 10 mph (16 kph), its humpback left ripples in the water, which are visible in the photographs.

CHAPTER 1
Sightings

"Let no one imagine that I either state a falsehood…or record anything doubtful or uncertain. Be it known that I will tell with all candor what I have learned from the consistent narrative of my predecessors, trustworthy and discerning men, and that my narrative is founded either on what I have been able to find recorded in the pages of those who have gone before me, or what I have learned in diligent inquiry, by hearing it from certain faithful old men, who have told me without hesitation." -St. Adamnan, *Life of St. Columba*

Far up in the north of Great Britain, surrounded by the rugged mountains of the Scottish Highlands, lies Loch Ness. Is this cold, dark lake the natural habitat of a huge creature not yet known to zoologists? Or—as skeptics maintain—is there nothing to back up the reported sightings but hysteria, bad science, and wishful thinking?

The story of the Loch Ness monster begins more than fourteen hundred years ago, in 565 AD. In that year, the Irish missionary Saint Columba had a dramatic encounter with a water monster. Columba's biographer, Saint Adamnan, tells the story

On another occasion also, when the blessed man was living for some days in the province of the Picts, he was obliged to cross the river Ness; and when he reached the bank of the river, he saw some of the inhabitants

Loch Ness has been the home of the enduring legend of the Loch Ness monster for decades.

burying an unfortunate man, who was a short time before seized as he was swimming, and bitten most severely by a monster that lived in the water. . . . The blessed man, on hearing this...directed one of his companions to swim over and row across the boat that was moored at the farther bank. . . . But the monster, which, so far from being satiated, was only roused for more prey, was lying at the bottom of the stream, and when it felt the water disturbed above by the man swimming, suddenly rushed out and, giving an awful roar, darted after him with its mouth wide open, as the man swam in the middle of the stream. Then the blessed man observing this, raised his holy hand. . . and commanded the ferocious monster, saying, "Thou shalt go no further, nor touch the man; go back with all speed." Then at the voice of the saint, the monster was terrified, and fled more quickly than if it had been pulled back with ropes.

Adamnan's story is interesting—but is it true? Adamnan himself undoubtedly believed it. But Adamnan wrote his *Life of St. Columba* over a century after Saint Columba's supposed meeting with the lake (or river) monster.

Also, the monster seen by Saint Columba is different in at least two ways from the creature described in modern reports. Saint Columba's monster makes "an awful roar," and it is a killer. The modern Loch Ness monster, on the other hand, makes no sounds and doesn't attack people. All that the story really tells us is that reports of a water monster near Loch Ness go back at least as far as the sixth century.

Murky Legends

Legends of water monsters were well known in the Highlands of Scotland. The kelpie, also known as the water horse, was a creature that lived in and about the lochs. The name "water horse" came from its habit of taking the appearance of a fine horse standing saddled and bridled by the roadside. Unfortunate travelers who tried to ride this horse would find themselves

At first, the Loch Ness monster was portrayed in a variety of forms, such as fantastical creatures. Only later, due to supposed photographic "evidence," did we gain the modern image of the creature.

stuck on its back, unable to let loose of the reins, as the creature plunged headlong into the nearby loch.

With the coming of the modern era, the stories about the Highland water horses grew less fantastical and more realistic. Gone were the enchanted bridles and the death plunges, but from time to time the occasional sighting of an unusual animal would still be reported in the local press.

For example, in 1802, a man named Alexander Macdonald saw a large stubby-legged animal surface and propel itself to within 50 yards (45 m) of where he stood on the shore of the loch. In 1880 another Macdonald—named Duncan this time—dove into the loch near Fort Augustus to inspect the keel of a wrecked ship. While he was down there he saw an animal like a huge frog lying on an underwater shelf of rock. And in 1926, the *Inverness Courier* reported that a Simon McGarry of Invergarry saw the gulls rise screaming into the air above the loch, and a creature emerge. "Before my eyes, something like an upturned boat rose from the depths, and I can still see the water cascading down its sides. Just as suddenly, though, it sank out of sight."

Then, in 1933, a highlander named Hugh Gray was walking beside the river near the village of Foyers when he saw a creature rolling about in the water. But this time was different. Hugh Gray was carrying a camera.

The Loch Ness Lakes

Loch Ness today is the largest of a series of glacial lakes running along the fault line of the Great Glen from Inverness to Fort William. The Loch Ness holds the greatest volume of fresh water in Great Britain.

A HISTORY OF LOCH NESS

Four hundred million years ago, in what would someday become the Scottish Highlands, part of the Caledonian Mountains slid more than 60 miles (96 km) to the south. The fault line left a mile-wide rift valley that still runs all the way across Scotland, from the North Sea to the Atlantic Ocean. This valley is Glen Mor, the Great Glen. Loch Ness lies in the northeasternmost portion of the Great Glen.

Over time the continents cracked apart and drifted. During the Age of Dinosaurs, long-necked plesiosaurs swam in the shallow seas that covered much of North America and Europe. Mammals arose, dinosaurs died off, the climate grew colder, and eventually ice sheets spread over much of the world.

During the Ice Age, glaciers covered the Scottish Highlands with a layer of ice up to 4,000 feet (1,219 m) deep. The ice pressed down on the land and caused the rock to sink beneath sea level. As the ice melted, the land rose. The portion of the rift valley that would become Loch Ness was an arm of the sea. The rising land, the falling sea level, and the melting glaciers worked together to cut off the loch from the ocean and replace the salt water with fresh water. The surface of the loch is now about 52 feet (15.8 m) above sea level.

The sides of the loch are steep, and the bottom of the loch is soft mud, flat and level. The rock walls of the loch extend below the mud in a V shape, and may go down as far as 900 feet (274.32 m). Not counting the mud and whatever lies below it, Loch Ness is the second-deepest lake in the British Isles, and the third-deepest lake in Europe. The River Ness, about 7 miles (11 km) long, drains the loch into the sea at Beauly Firth. The Highland city of Inverness is located on the river, between Loch Ness and the sea.

The waters of Loch Ness are dark and cold, murky with particles of peat moss washed in by the streams that feed the loch. The sun warms the upper levels of the loch, down to about 150 feet (45.72 m). Below 150 feet the water maintains a constant temperature near 45 degrees Fahrenheit (7.2° Celsius). The loch never freezes over in the coldest Highland winters.

Humans came into the Great Glen area around 6,000 years ago. The first settlers were the Picts, whose name comes from the Latin *Picti*, or "painted people," a nickname the Romans gave them because of their fondness for tattoos and body paint.

In the Past

From the Middle Ages on through the beginning of the modern era, war and violence marked the countryside around the loch. In the 11th century, Macbeth supposedly murdered King Duncan while the king was a guest at Macbeth's castle about a half-mile northeast of Inverness. Bonnie Prince Charlie's defeat in 1746 at the Battle of Culloden, 7 miles (11 km) south of Inverness, spelled the end of Scottish independence.

Over the next century modern agriculture and the desire for wealth finished what warfare had started. For centuries the Highlanders had lived by small-scale agriculture and cattle raising, but in the late 1700s the great landowners began changing over to large-scale sheep farming. To make room for flocks of sheep, the landowners forcibly evicted their own tenant farmers. The Highland Clearances, as the process was called, lasted into the nineteenth century.

The Caledonian Canal, begun in 1803, opened the Great Glen to commerce. By the early years of the twentieth century Inverness had become a popular tourist destination, reachable by train. In 1933—the same year that Hugh Gray took his walk by the river—the Loch Ness road finally opened the banks of the loch to automobile traffic.

CHAPTER 2
A Monster Takes Shape

s there a large animal in Loch Ness? Between the time when Saint Columba dismissed a monster with his word and when Hugh Grey snapped his photo, there are perhaps two dozen mentions of a creature in the Loch. The monster usually takes one of three forms. The first and most common is the moving wake, a pattern of waves in the water of the loch that hints at the presence of something large swimming just beneath. The second is a humped body, either moving or stationary, rising above the water. The third, and rarest, form is a long neck with a small head.

With its remoteness and air of mystery, the Scottish Highlands are a perfect setting for the legend of the Loch Ness monster.

But could an undiscovered animal as large as the Loch Ness monster possibly exist? The answer is yes. Animals previously unknown to science have been found more than once in the past hundred years. For instance, there's the megamouth shark (*Megachasma pelagios*), a 15-foot (4.6 m) long creature

UNANSWERED QUESTIONS

There is no reason to suppose that all the monster sightings have the same cause. Nor is there any reason to rule out a large, unknown animal as one of the causes. As of this moment, we just don't know. The Smithsonian Institute says: "Even though most scientists believe the likelihood of a monster is small, they keep an open mind as scientists should and wait for concrete proof in the form of skeletal evidence or the actual capture of such a creature." Until then, observers on the shore will keep on looking for a rippled wake, or a humped back, or a long-necked creature rising out of the depths—and the waters of Loch Ness will keep their secrets.

weighing nearly a ton. The first specimen was discovered on November 15, 1976, when it was found entangled in the drag anchor of a U.S. Navy ship. The new creature wasn't described scientifically until 1983. Twelve years after the first sighting, only three specimens had been found. Since that time, fewer than twenty megamouth sharks have been captured, or even seen. The megamouth remains the only species in its genus, and the only genus in its order.

There's also the pseudo-oryx, a large antelope discovered in Southeast Asia in 1992. Local inhabitants, of course, had always known about the animal. It was merely mainstream science that hadn't gotten the word. Other animals once thought to be legendary that have been proved to exist within the last hundred years include the giant panda and the Kodiak bear.

Sometimes creatures thought to have vanished long ago have been rediscovered. The coelacanth, an ancient fish, was known only from the fossil record. Scientists thought that the species had died out some 400 million years ago. Then, in 1938, a fisherman caught a coelacanth off the coast of Africa. A second one turned up in 1952, and others have been seen since.

A Timeline of Sightings

Could the reports of a Loch Ness monster be a case of "no smoke without fire"? Let's take a look at some of the smoke.

On July 22, 1930, three young men from Inverness were fishing from a boat near Dores. They sighted a disturbance in the water that commenced about 600 yards (548.64 m) away from them, moved toward them at about 15 knots until it came to within 300 yards (274 m), with a part protruding

Inverness Castle overlooks the River Ness in Inverness, Scotland, the reputed home of the enduring legend.

from the water being 20 feet (6 m) long by 3 feet (.9 m) high.

On April 14, 1933, the Mackays were driving along the side of Loch Ness on the new road from Inverness. Near the town of Abriachan, Mrs. Mackay spotted "an enormous animal rolling and plunging" in the center of the loch.

The *Daily Express*, a Glasgow newspaper, reported on June 9, 1933: "Mystery fish in Scottish loch. Monster reported at Fort Augustus. A monster fish which for years has been somewhat of a mystery in Loch Ness was reported to have been seen yesterday at Fort Augustus."

On October 23, 1933, the London *Daily Mail* reported from Scotland: "In Inverness, the Highland Capital, there is one topic of conversation— 'the beast' as by one accord everybody dubs the uncanny denizen of the loch by this sinister title. Some think the loch harbors a survivor of some prehistoric creature which may have been released from the earth's recesses by the great blasting operations required for the making of the new Inverness-Glasgow motor road."

On October 29, 1933, E. G. Boulenger, the director of the aquarium at the London Zoo, sounded a word of caution: "The case of the Monster in Loch Ness is worthy of our consideration if only because it presents a striking example of mass hallucination."

On November 13, 1933, the same day on which Gray snapped his photo, the government became involved. Sir Murdoch Macdonald, representing Inverness-shire in Parliament, wrote to the Secretary of State for Scotland: "As no doubt you are aware, some animal or fish of an unusual kind has found its way into Loch Ness. I think I can say the evidence of its presence can be taken as undoubted. Far too many people have seen something abnormal to question its existence. So far, there has been no indication of its being a harmful animal or fish, and until somebody states the genus to which it belongs, I do hope you can authorise the police in the district to prevent pothunters deliberately looking for it."

But the tales of the Loch Ness monster proved to be more than just a seven-day-wonder and a silly-season newspaper flash. By one count, over four thousand eyewitness accounts of an unusual animal in Loch Ness have appeared since 1933, eleven of them in the year 2000.

CHAPTER 3
The Case of the Mysterious Photos

Loch Ness is big. An observer standing at the water line and looking across the loch will find that the opposite shore is halfway to the horizon. Looking lengthwise down the loch, the same observer would not be able to see the far end at all.

Weather conditions at the loch are extreme. The weather station at Fort Augustus, in the period from 1920 to 1950, reported fewer sunny days than any other station in Britain. The wind howls up the Great Glen, whipping the surface of the loch to foam where a moment before the water

The megamouth shark *(Megachasma pelagios)* is one of a number of creatures that are relatively new to science. Its recent capture adds to the hope that a Loch Ness monster will eventually be discovered.

had been still and glassy. Observation is even trickier during twilight, and the high northern latitude of Scotland produces long twilights.

Making observations across open water is difficult at best. Estimating size and distance is hard without familiar objects near the unknown to provide a scale. Open water is also prone to mirage conditions. A floating log, a bird, a distant boat, a wind-blown wave, a deer swimming in the loch—any of these things, seen under the right lighting conditions, could be misinterpreted as a fabulous monster. Furthermore, human memories are fallible. People see what they want to see, and remember what they want to remember.

The Skeptics

A less charitable interpretation is that there was no creature at all, and that it was only after seeing a blurred and indistinct picture on the developed film

Creatures previously thought to be extinct, such as this coelacanth fish captured in 2007, only fuel the speculation about a possible Loch Ness monster.

that Gray came up with a story to sell to the press. Some people who look at the photo see the head of a dog with a stick in its mouth, swimming toward the camera. Others see other creatures, which all seem to fit the various authors' several theories.

Matters were not helped when the next piece of hard evidence turned out to be a provable hoax. The London *Daily Mail* hired a professional big-game hunter to go to Loch Ness and bring back evidence of the creature's existence. The hunter, Marmaduke "Duke" Wetherall, arrived in

EVIDENCE?

When arguing for the existence of the Loch Ness monster, we must turn to the photos for our evidence. But can we rely on the photos as evidence? That is, are they real? Let's look at Hugh Gray's photo first. It is, at best, a blurry shot of something unidentifiable. There are no foreground objects with which to make a size comparison. Gray estimated the object to be 200 yards (182.88 m) away. An ordinary camera is hard-pressed to take detailed photos at that range. Gray stated that the object was obscured by spray, that it was dark gray in color, and that it stood 3 to 4 feet (.9 to 1.2 m) out of the water. He took five shots with his camera, then went home.

And there his camera, with what could be astounding pictures inside, lay untouched for two weeks. The most charitable interpretation this delay is the one Gray himself gives—he was afraid that nothing would appear on the film, and that he would be kidded by his fellow workers. When the film was at last developed, four of the five shots showed nothing, and the fifth showed what seemed to be a creature with its head underwater, the tail farthest from the photographer.

mid-December of 1933. Within a few days Wetherall had found mysterious footprints on the shores of the loch. He dutifully made a plaster cast and sent it back to London for identification, all amidst great publicity. And amid great publicity came the answer, issued from the British Museum of Natural History on January 4, 1934: the footprints were all made by the right rear foot of a female hippopotamus. Stuffed. Someone had apparently used a hippopotamus-foot umbrella stand to create the "monster" footprints, and Wetherall had fallen for it.

Instantly, the Loch Ness monster became a laughingstock that no legitimate scientist could touch and come away with his reputation intact. Forty years later, when the Academy of Applied Science launched an expedition to the loch in an attempt to take underwater photos of the creature, it would be mocked by the comic strip "Doonesbury" as "the Academy of Implied Science." Wetherall stated that in his opinion the loch contained nothing more than a large gray seal. The publicity started to fade.

A Turning Point

Then came April 1934. On the nineteenth of that month, R. K. Wilson, a respected London surgeon, was on holiday in Scotland. Around 7:00 in the morning, Wilson stopped about 2 miles (3 km) north of Invermoriston. There, "I had got over the dyke and was standing a few yards down the slope and looking towards the loch when I noticed a considerable commotion on the surface some distance out from the shore, perhaps two or three hundred yards (274 meters) out. I watched it for perhaps a minute or so and saw something break the surface. My friend shouted: 'My God, it's the Monster!'

Wilson stated: "I ran the few yards to the car and got the camera and then went down and along the steep bank for about fifty yards to where my friend was and got the camera focused on something which was moving through the water. I could not say what this object was as I was far too busy managing the camera in my amateurish way."

Wilson took four photos, which he brought to be developed that same day in Inverness. The pictures came back that afternoon. The first two were blank; the third showed what appeared to be a head and neck rising above the water. The fourth showed the creature sinking back into the loch.

That third, best-known photo is certainly startling. If this is indeed the head and neck of a creature extending 4 feet (1.2 m) above the surface of the loch, it resembles nothing so much as a plesiosaur, a carnivorous aquatic reptile thought to have become extinct some sixty five million years ago.

CHAPTER 4
The Mystery Deepens

Wilson sold the head-and-neck picture to the *Daily Mail* on his return to London and created an instant sensation. For some people, the photograph proved the existence of an unknown animal. Others weren't so sure.

When a picture of an unknown object has no objects of known size in the foreground, the exact size of the unknown can't be determined. In this case, rather than seeing a large object a long way away, some people saw a small object close by: a water bird,

Grainy photographs are the only "evidence" we have of the Loch Ness monster. Their low-quality nature only raises skepticism about their authenticity.

the tail of a diving otter, or a floating log with a root sticking above the water.

One of the objections to the photo is that while Wilson said that the thing he photographed was moving, the ripples on the water show it to be stationary. Perhaps, some say, it was moving, but had stopped by the time he got his camera to his eye. Perhaps, others suggest, it was never moving at all.

The second photo, the one the newspaper didn't run, is of far poorer quality than the famous shot. Nevertheless, it has some interesting features. One is that the angle between the "head" and the "neck" of the object has changed. It's

Doubters continue to analyze the details of the few photos of the Loch Ness monster, such as the ripples in the water, to try to uncover a hoax.

unlikely that a tree root would make such a change.

Theories of a Hoax

On March 13, 1994, the London *Sunday Telegraph* ran a story claiming that the famous photo was actually a picture of an 18-inch (45.72 cm) model, and that Wilson had not taken the photos himself, but had allowed his name and reputation to be used for the occasion. According to the *Sunday Telegraph*, a man named Christian Spurling had confessed to perpetrating a hoax sixty years before at the urging of his stepfather—none other than "Duke" Wetherall, the big-game hunter who had himself been hoaxed by the dried hippo foot.

WHAT DO WE KNOW SCIENTIFICALLY?

Science works, first, by collecting the available information, or data, about the thing being studied. Second, scientists take this information and try to come up with a hypothesis that explains how the data fits together. Third, they devise experiments to test those hypotheses. Once a hypothesis is verified by the experimental method, it becomes a theory.

Along the way there are several general principles. One is called Occam's razor, after William of Occam, a medieval monk and early scientist who said, "Logical entities should not be multiplied unnecessarily." Another way of putting that is, "If you have two competing theories that make exactly the same predictions, the one that is simpler is the better."

The least complex theory may still be quite complex. As Albert Einstein put it, "Everything should be made as simple as possible, but not simpler."

Given two hypotheses, one that "the sightings of unidentified objects in Loch Ness are caused by unknown animals seen at great distances under bad light conditions" and the second that "the sightings of unidentified objects in Loch Ness are caused by floating logs seen at great distances under bad light conditions," the log explanation is simpler. We already know, by other means, that there are floating logs in the loch.

Is there a reasonable way to prove that the loch (or, indeed, any body of water) is monster-free? If a search fails to find any monsters, then perhaps the search was in the wrong location, at the wrong time, or using the wrong means. If one photo turns out to be a fake, that doesn't mean that the next photo won't be real. If one observer is mistaken, that

Skeptics of the Loch Ness monster turn to the philosophy of William of Occam, a medieval monk who suggested that, all things being equal, the simplest answer is most often correct.

doesn't mean the next observer won't be completely accurate. The people who claim that there is a large, unknown animal in Loch Ness are the ones who have to provide the proof that there really is one. Extraordinary claims require extraordinary proof. Show us the proof, the skeptics say. Give us a monster we can study in the flesh.

By the time Spurling told his story, everyone else supposedly involved in the hoax was dead. And by the time the story was printed, Spurling himself was dead at the age of ninety. All anyone can say for certain, therefore, is that either Spurling was fibbing, or that Wilson was.

CHAPTER 5

Hunting for "Nessie"

The history of the Loch Ness monster continued after R. K. Wilson sold his picture to the *Daily Mail*. In the summer of 1934, Sir Edward Mountain, a gentleman described as "an enthusiastic angler," rented Beaufort Castle on Loch Ness and spent the month of July hunting for evidence of a creature. He hired twenty men and posted them a mile or so apart down the 24-mile (38.6 km) length of the loch. Each man had binoculars and a camera, and watched from 8 AM to 6 PM. The men reported back every night on what they had seen. Sir Edward marked each sighting on a map of the loch. In two weeks of good weather, the watchers claimed to have sighted what could be a creature no fewer than twenty-one times and took five photos. Then bad weather set in, and the sightings stopped. The five photos were "disappointing," lacking even the detail of the London surgeon's photo. No conclusions could be drawn.

Sir Edward switched to one man with a movie camera and a telephoto lens. This eventually yielded movie footage of something later identified by zoologists as a large seal, the same conclusion that Wetherall had reached earlier that year. Sir Edward's film has since been lost.

During WWII, the loch came under the control of the Royal Navy. The monster was forgotten. Then in 1951, a worker for the Forestry Commission named Lachlan Steuart saw what he first thought was a large motorboat speeding down the loch. Realizing that it was no motorboat, he grabbed a camera and took a photograph of a three-humped creature that he estimated to be about 57 feet (17.4 m) long from noise to tail.

What kind of creature might have such a shape is difficult to imagine. Some people see not one creature, but three in a pack traveling together. Others claim that the photo shows three hay bales floating in the loch, and that Steuart was either mistaken or fibbing when he claimed that he saw them move.

There matters might have stood, but new evidence from another source turned up. On December 2, 1954, a fishing boat named *Rival III* out of Peterhead was passing down the loch when something unusual turned up on the echosounder. The device showed an object off Urquhart Bay, 480 feet

Traditionally, archaeologists use physical evidence to study ancient creatures, such as these mastodon bones. Without such evidence for the Loch Ness monster, there's only speculation.

(146.3 m) down, 120 feet (36.5 m) above the bottom of the loch. Experts who later examined the trace stated that the echo wasn't the result of a mechanical malfunction from the machine, that it hadn't been tampered with, and that the object wasn't a waterlogged tree or a shoal of fish.

Sonar Technology

Sonar continues to be used to search the loch, although with inconclusive results. We know a lot more about the loch now—we know that the water under the thermocline, once thought to be devoid of life, actually has an 80 percent oxygen saturation, and that fish live there down to the bottom,

FINDING "NESSIE" WITH SCIENCE

More sonar evidence turned up over the following years. In 1968, the University of Birmingham, using shore-mounted sonar, detected and recorded a large unknown object traveling in the loch. Some sonar searches have been disappointing. If identifying an animal from a blurry photograph is difficult, identifying one from a sonar echo is more so. The nearly vertical, parallel stone sides of Loch Ness, combined with the thermocline (a boundary between water layers of different temperatures) at 150 feet (45.72 m) down, produce difficult conditions for sonar operation. Sonar signals are bent or reflected when they hit a thermocline—submarines use this fact to hide from sonar searches.

In 1976, Christopher McGowan and Martin Klein searched the bottom of Loch Ness for the bones of a monster, using towed side-scan sonar. The system had found mastodon bones on the bottom of a lake in New Hampshire during a test run. But, while they found the remains of a crashed WWII aircraft in Loch Ness, and Pictish stone circles beneath the current water line, no monster bones turned up. However, McGowan and Klein only searched the shallow areas of the loch.

In 1982, months of patrolling with scanning sonar produced forty hits on objects larger than the largest known fish, which could not be explained as false signals.

In 1987, Operation Deepscan was mounted. It consisted of nineteen boats sailing side by side, sweeping the loch from wall to wall with a curtain of sound. They sailed the long way down the loch, once each way, during the two-day search. Numerous strong sonar echoes "larger than a shark but smaller than a whale" were recorded. They all appeared to be moving, and many were below 150 feet (45.72 m). Yet problems abounded with this search, too. The sonar systems mounted on the boats interfered with each other, so they had to be set to their lowest power. At the end of the two-day sweep, all the expedition organizers had was a set of returns that they couldn't identify.

where arctic char and lampreys swim in the blackness. But so far, no unknown animals have been brought to the surface.

While the sonar searches went on, surface observation and photography continued. In 1960, a man named Tim Dinsdale took a movie of an unknown object in the loch. Some claim that it was a motorboat seen at a great distance under poor lighting conditions. But when the film was analyzed by Britain's Joint Air Reconnaissance Intelligence Center (JARIC) in 1966, the RAF's photographic experts said that what the film showed was "probably an animate object."

Some people believe that the Loch Ness monster could be related to the plesiosaur, an ancient aquatic creature that lived at the time of the dinosaurs.

During the years 1962–1972, a group called the Loch Ness Phenomena Investigation Bureau ringed the loch with movie and still cameras fitted with telephoto lenses in an attempt to duplicate one or more of the classic monster photos. They were unable to do so. While they did get some photos of objects that could not be identified, they did not get any photos of objects that were definitely an unknown animal.

The Academy of Applied Sciences, an American group, launched an investigation of its own in the early 1970s, financed in part by the *New York Times* and the National Geographic Society. The expedition was led by Dr. Robert Rines. The equipment was designed by Harold "Doc" Edgerton, a professor at Massachusetts Institute of Technology and the inventor of both strobe photography and side-scan sonar. When computer enhanced, the underwater photos they took seemed to show a large five-sided fin, and—in another photo—the head and neck of an unknown animal.

"None of the photographs is sufficiently informative to establish the existence, far less the identity, of a large animal in the loch," a team of experts from the British Museum of Natural History said in November 1975. "To one of us it strongly suggested the head of a horse with a bridle, and others conceded this likeness when it was pointed out. The size limits are compatible with this explanation. On this interpretation, eyes, ears, noseband, and nostrils are visible, along with a less clear structure that could represent a neck. We believe that the image is too imprecise for us to argue that this does indeed represent a dead horse, but we equally believe that such an interpretation cannot be eliminated."

Unfortunately, the murky water of the loch made the underwater photos blurry and dim, and when others tried to computer enhance the original photos, they did not get the same results that the academy did. Other investigations followed, with sonar, with surface and subsurface cameras, and even with small submarines. In the summer of 2000, a Swedish businessman asked for permission to cruise the loch with a specially modified crossbow in an attempt to get a skin sample from the unknown animal so that DNA testing

The "tully monster" is another creature that some suggest could be related to the Loch Ness monster though, like the plesiosaur, it's known to be extinct.

could show what it was. He was refused permission on the grounds that Scottish law forbids annoying livestock.

What, Then, Is in Loch Ness?

Hypotheses abound. None of them are strong enough to make it up to the status of a theory. Assuming there is a creature, is it a mammal? Whales, seals, and giant otters have all been suggested—but sea mammals tend to be friendly and gregarious. They come up frequently for air, and on cold days their breath is visible. A family of whales spouting in the loch wouldn't remain mysterious for long.

How about a reptile? The extinct plesiosaur looks like the Loch Ness monster of legend. The water in the loch is cold, but it never freezes, and the leatherback turtle, an ocean-dwelling reptile, lives in the waters off Scotland.

But reptiles also need to come to the surface for air. Furthermore, it would be astonishing if a breeding population of plesiosaurs had survived undetected for sixty-five million years.

An amphibian, then? Amphibians' bodies sink when they die, and some amphibians maintain gills all their lives. They might never need to come to the surface. Duncan Macdonald, the diver who saw something underwater in 1880, described what he saw as looking like a frog. But amphibians lay egg masses, and no such eggs have been seen in the loch.

How about a fish? Sturgeon can grow quite large and are certainly odd-looking creatures. But sturgeon don't have long necks or a tendency to come to the surface.

A large invertebrate, with no fixed body shape, could supply the wide variety of forms attributed to the Loch Ness monster. Some writers have suggested that the long "neck" of the Loch Ness creature is a single tentacle of a giant squid, raised above the surface for a moment. One researcher suggested that the Loch Ness creature is a "tully monster." Unfortunately, the tully monster, like the plesiosaur, is long extinct—and its largest fossil is only a few centimeters long.

Suppose there isn't a living creature at all? What else could people have been reporting? Boats, birds, and floating logs, seen at a great distance under poor lighting conditions, have all been suggested—but these explanations don't explain the close-up sightings.

How about mirages? W. H. Lehn of the Department of Electrical Engineering at the University of Manitoba published an article, "Atmospheric

Refraction and Lake Monsters," in *Science* magazine, 1979. He demonstrated that the refraction effect of layers of air at different temperatures could make logs and similar objects appear to stretch upward and transform into long-necked "monsters." Cold, deep Loch Ness is ideal for producing inversion layers of the kind that Lehn suggests. But mirages don't alarm seabirds, and they don't create moving wakes that break on the shore.

Something that might produce waves breaking on shore without wind or a passing boat is minor earthquake activity. Loch Ness is in an active geologic fault. A temblor could certainly alarm seabirds.

Others have speculated that the hump rising from the surface of the loch is a mat of rotting vegetation, lifted by methane gas, which sinks again after the gas bubble bursts into the air. We do know that there are two areas on the bottom of the loch—one off Fort Augustus, one off Urquhart Castle—that produce methane. But no such mats of vegetation have washed ashore.

CHAPTER 6

The Loch Ness Monster in Popular Culture

A reason why the Loch Ness monster has captured the public's attention for so many years is that it serves our need to answer the unexplainable. Nearly every society is captured by a similar mystery. Whether it is the Loch Ness monster, Big Foot, ghosts and poltergeists, the Bermuda Triangle, or UFOs, these unexplained phenomena give us a reason to keep

Authors such as J. K. Rowling have used the legend of the Loch Ness monster in their stories.

asking questions and to satisfy our need to solve our mysteries. For this reason, the Loch Ness monster has survived in popular culture such as literature, movies, television, and comic books.

Loch Ness in Literature

The Loch Ness monster has appeared in literature for many years. Since the 1950, there have been dozens of works written on the subject in magazines, newspapers, and books, including by such popular authors as J. K. Rowling, author of the Harry Potter series of young adult books. Interestingly, much of what is written is done so as nonfiction, even though the creature itself has still not yet been proven to exist.

In 1959, the British mystery author and screenwriter Leslie Charteris penned the short story "The Convenient Monster," whose main character Simon Templar investigates an alleged monster attack. The roots of the story have many parallels with the story of the Loch Ness monster:

Though the actual Loch Ness monster doesn't appear in Charteris' story, there are many works of literature in which it does. In the 1977 book *The Mysterious Tadpole*, a boy receives a tadpole for his birthday and soon discovers that it is the offspring of the creature. In Susan Cooper's 1997 novel *The Boggart and the Monster*, the Loch Ness monster appears as a shape shifter. Finally, in J. K. Rowling's 2001 story *Fantastic Beasts and Where to Find Them*, the monster is actually discovered to be a supernatural water horse from Celtic folklore.

The Loch Ness Monster in Folklore

Before movies and television, the Loch Ness monster appeared in the public consciousness in the medium of the day: folklore. The monster was often associated with the legends of mystical lake creatures called kelpies. Kelpies were first described as being horselike and appeared out of the surface of the water. These tales served a distinct purpose to keep children away from and out of the lake.

More modern accounts of the Loch Ness monster made them appear more like plesiosaurs, an aquatic reptile that lived at the time of the dinosaurs, which were unknown at the time of the kelpie. Describing the monster as resembling plesiosaurs gives the monster a more realistic and credible identity. People are more apt to relate to a creature that they have seen a likeness of and know existed in the past.

Whatever the origins, tales of the Loch Ness have been told for generations and will continue to be. While the means of storytelling may change, the story itself remains the same.

Movies

Given its cult-icon status, the Loch Ness monster is a perfect candidate for portrayal in cinema of all genres, including horror, thriller, suspense, and even comedy.

Since the early twentieth century, virtually in the infancy of the cinema, up until today, the Loch Ness monster has been a star.

The first picture to use the Loch Ness monster as a subject was the 1934 film *The Secret of the Loch*, which filmed a water snake and used special effects to turn it into the infamous character we all know. Though this first portrayal of the monster in film was more or less straightforward, offering the literal story line of the account of the creature, future filmmakers would grow considerably more creative in the portrayal in years to come.

In the second half of the century, "Nessie" appeared in the 1961 film *What a Whopper*, a British comedy written by Terry Nation, about a group of Englishmen who travel to the famous lake to fake sightings about the monster. This account of the monster reflected the growing intrigue with the mystery. On a certain level, *What a Whopper* quenched the public's thirst for an answer to the mystery. Going so far as to fake an account of a sighting, though fictional, offered a mild, and temporary, answer to the unanswered.

In 1981 the character appeared in *The Loch Ness Horror*, directed by Larry Buchanan. The creature plays a central role in this film, going on a killing spree by feeding on unsuspecting swimmers. Adding to the monster's mystique, in

Even legendary directors such as Billy Wilder used the Loch Ness monster, which appeared as a character in his film *The Private Life of Sherlock Holmes*.

the 1987 movie *Amazon Women on the Moon*, the Loch Ness monster was speculated to be the famous serial killer Jack the Ripper.

Mentioning the monster's comedic role in film, the monster appeared in the Billy Wilder film *The Private Life of Sherlock Holmes*. Wilder, known for his classics *Some Like It Hot* and *The Apartment*, creatively used the Loch Ness monster as a character in *The Private Life of Sherlock Holmes* in a scene where Holmes' sidekick, Watson, apparently spots the creature. While the figure plays just a small part in the movie, its appearance itself is a testament to the mystique of the creature.

Using comedy to portray this mysterious and scary creature allows the public to see the Loch Ness monster in a softer light. Instead of approaching it, and any fearsome creature for that matter, as something to run away from, comedy allows us to embrace that which is unknown or unknowable. This is much like the way humans use humor to talk about sensitive topics. Filmmakers used comedy to portray this mysterious creature.

The Loch Ness monster has even appeared in animated movies, such as the 1992 picture *Freddie* as F.R.0.7. In the tale, Nessie is freed from under a boulder by a frog prince, Frederick. Later, the monster repays the favor by helping Frederick defeat invaders of Britain.

Other films in which Nessie has appeared are the *Loch Ness* (1996) starring Ted Danson; *Beneath Loch Ness* (2001); *Monsters, Inc.* (2001); *Scooby-Doo and the Loch Ness Monster* (2004); *Napoleon Dynamite* (2004); *Incident at Loch Ness* (2004); *The Water Horse: Legend of the Deep* (2007); and most recently, *Beyond Loch Ness* (2008).

The appearance of the Loch Ness monster in cinema over such a large span of time—virtually that of the existence of movies—is a testament to the enduring mystique of the legend. In addition, the ability for the creature to be portrayed in such a wide range of types of movies, from horror to comedy, shows how versatile the legend is.

Television

Television is quite appropriate for stories of the Loch Ness monster. Since the legend is burned in the minds of most people and since it is a myth that seems to never lose momentum, there are countless ways the myth can be weaved into the brief plots of television story lines.

Take, for instance, a 1971 episode of *Bewitched* called "Samantha and the Loch Ness Monster." The creature is portrayed as a warlock upon whom a spell is cast. In the 1975 *Doctor Who* episode "Terror of the Zygons," the creature is viewed as an alien cyborg that needs to be slain. In these two portrayals, Nessie is portrayed as an evil force that needs to be protected against, which supports our fears about the mystery of the creature. Even though there is no scientific evidence that the Loch Ness monster exists aside from some grainy photographs, we as a society still are intimidated by the unknown.

On the other side of the coin are portrayals of the Loch Ness monster in a humorous light. The British television series *The Family-Ness* portrayed the adventures of the monster's family along with their human friends, just as

Matt Groening, creator of *The Simpsons* animated series, has used the Loch Ness monster as a character in the television show.

traditional families are portrayed in standard sitcoms. In *The Simpsons* episode "Money Can't Buy Me Love," the Loch Ness monster is captured and eventually goes to work at a casino.

In one episode of *How I Met Your Mother*, the character of Marshall feels that the "monster" is portrayed unfairly and that it is in fact a gentle creature," spending a week and a half looking for it on his honeymoon. The monster even made an appearance in an anime cartoon, *Sherlock Hound*. The creature appears at the end of the episode "The Adventure of the Three Students."

In another animated series, *Happy Ness: The Secret of the Loch*, multiple Loch Ness monsters appear with comical names such as Happy Ness, Forgetful Ness, and Silly Ness. These were considered the good "Nessies." The bad ones, or villains, were named "Pompous Ness," "Mean Ness," and "Dark Ness." Other play on names and words in the series were "Loch-ets," which they used to perform a "Ness Bless," which cast a spell on whomever it struck. The "Loch-ets" also enabled the wearer to become invisible if necessary.

Nessie has also appeared in the cartoon comedy *South Park*. In the episode "The Succubus," the monster is comically portrayed as a beggar asking for three dollars and fifty cents, using disguises such as a Girl Scout selling cookies to obtain the money.

GLOSSARY

archaeologist A scientist who studies fossils and bones of creatures that lived long ago.

cult icon Any entity that gains a dedicated following based on fantastical stories.

data Information about something being studied.

echosounder A device that locates underwater objects by bouncing sound waves off them.

experiment A scientific test conducted to come to a proven conclusion.

highlands The mountainous area of northern Scotland.

hypothesis A proposed idea of how data fits together.

kelpie A dangerous horse-shaped water monster in Scottish folklore.

Lake Ness The third deepest lake in Europe and possibly the home of one or more "monsters."

loch The Irish and Scottish Gaelic term for lake.

Nessie Nickname for the Loch Ness monster.

plesiosaur A long-necked aquatic reptile that lived during the time of the dinosaurs. It's been suggested that the Loch Ness monster might be one.

theory A hypothesis that has been verified by scientific experiments.

thermocline A boundary between water layers of different temperatures.

tully monster Also known as *Tullimonstrum gregarium*, this creature was an invertebrate that lived in shallow tropical waters 300 million years ago.

zoologist A scientist who studies animals.

FOR MORE INFORMATION

3D Loch Ness Experience

1 Parliament Square

Royal Mile

Edinburgh

EH1 1RE

0131 225 2290

Web site: http://www.3dlochness.com

The 3D Loch Ness Experience offers viewers an experience of the famous
mystery as up close as you can get by using 3-D technology to tell the tale.

About.com

Paranormal Phenomena

The New York Times Company

620 Eighth Avenue

New York, NY 10018

Web site: http://paranormal.about.com

There is a section of the information site that deals specifically with everything
paranormal.

Atlantic Paranormal Society

2362 West Shore Road

Warwick, RI 02889

Web site: http://the-atlantic-paranormal-society.com

This organization is committed to investigating paranormal activities.

The Beast of Loch Ness
Public Broadcasting Service
2100 Crystal Drive
Arlington, VA 22202
Web site: http://www.pbs.org/wgbh/nova/lochness
The Beast of Loch Ness is a presentation created by the PBS television show
    NOVA that explores the mystique surrounding this mysterious creature.

Loch Ness Discovery Centre
1 Parliament Square
High Street
Edinburgh
EH1 1RE
+44(0)131 226 1414
Web site: http://www.highlandexperience.com
The Loch Ness Discovery Centre offers information and tours of lands where
    the legend exits: Loch Ness, Inverness, and the Highlands of Scotland.

Loch Ness Exhibition Centre
Drumnadrochit
Loch Ness
Inverness-shire
IV63 6TU
Tel +44 (0) 1456 450573

Web site: http://www.lochness.com

The Loch Ness Exhibition Centre provides visitors with comprehensive information about the legend, the people, and the culture of Loch Ness and its surroundings.

Web Sites

Due to the changing nature of Internet links, Rosen Publishing has developed an online list of Web sites related to the subject of this book. This site is updated regularly. Please use this link to access the list:

http://www.rosenlinks.com/me/loch

FOR FURTHER READING

Alexander, John B. *UFOs: Myths, Conspiracies, and Realities.* New York, NY: Thomas Dunne, 2011.

Bord, Janet, Colin Bord, Loren Coleman, and Janet Bord. *Bigfoot Casebook Updated: Sightings and Encounters from 1818 to 2004.* Enumclaw, WA: Pine Winds, 2006.

Childress, David Hatcher. *Yetis, Sasquatch & Hairy Giants.* Kemptom, IL: Adventures Unlimited, 2010.

Emmer, Rick. *Loch Ness Monster: Fact or Fiction?* New York, NY: Chelsea House, 2010.

Imbrogno, Philip J. *Files from the Edge: A Paranormal Investigator's Explorations into High Strangeness.* Woodbury, MN: Llewellyn Publications, 2010.

Jack, Albert. *Loch Ness Monsters and Raining Frogs: The World's Most Puzzling Mysteries Solved.* New York, NY: Random House, 2009.

Kean, Leslie. *UFOs: Generals, Pilots, and Government Officials Go on the Record.* New York, NY: Harmony, 2010.

Kirkpatrick, Betty. *Nessie: The Legend of the Loch Ness Monster.* Edinburgh: Crombie Jardine, 2005.

Kitei, Lynne D. *The Phoenix Lights: A Skeptic's Discovery That We Are Not Alone.* Charlottesville, VA: Hampton Roads, 2010.

Miller, Connie Colwell. *The Loch Ness Monster: The Unsolved Mystery.* Mankato, MN: Capstone, 2009.

Randle, Kevin D. *Crash: When UFOs Fall from the Sky : A History of Famous Incidents, Conspiracies, and Cover-ups.* Franklin Lakes, NJ: New Page, 2010.

Redfern, Nicholas. *The NASA Conspiracies: The Truth Behind the Moon Landings, Censored Photos, and the Face on Mars.* Pompton Plains, NJ: New Page, 2011.

Schach, David. *The Loch Ness Monster.* Minneapolis, MN: Bellwether Media, 2010.

Starr, William W. *Whisky, Kilts, and the Loch Ness Monster: Traveling Through Scotland with Boswell and Johnson.* Columbia, SC: University of South Carolina, 2011.

Townsend, John. *Bigfoot and Other Mysterious Creatures.* St. Catharines, ON: Crabtree, 2009.

Vallee, Jacques. *Dimensions: A Casebook of Alien Contact.* San Antonio, TX: Anomalist, 2008.

Westwood, Jennifer, and Sophia Kingshill. *The Lore of Scotland: A Guide to Scottish Legends.* New York, NY: Random House, 2009.

INDEX

About the Authors

Nikki Case is an author living in New Jersey.

Martin Delrio is an author living in New York.

Photo Credits

Cover, pp. 1, 8–9 interior backgrounds Diane McDonald/Photographer's Choice RF/Getty Images; cover, back cover, p. 1 (lens) © www.istockphoto.com/jsemeniuk; cover (inset), back cover (inset), pp. 1 (inset), 32–33 Keystone/Hulton Archive/Getty Images; p. 5 (inset) Cascade News; pp. 5 (background), 7, 16, 23, 29, 36, 46 Shutterstock; pp. 11–12 © Mary Evans Picture Library/The Image Works; pp. 13, 18, 26, 34, 35, 39, 40, 49; p. 17 Time-Life Pictures/Getty Images; pp. 20–21 Anik Messier/Flickr/Getty Images; p. 24 Dorling Kindersley/The Agency Collection/Getty Images; p. 25 AFP/Getty Images; pp. 30–31 Alfred Geschedt/Photographer's Choice/Getty Images; pp. 32–33, 35 (inset) The Granger Collection; p. 38 David McNew/Getty Images Sport/Getty Images; p. 41 Christian Darkin/Photo Researchers; p. 43 © AP Images; p. 47 Chip Somodevilla/Getty Images News/Getty Images; p. 51 Bob Laundry/Time & Life Images/Time & Life Pictures/Getty Images; p. 54 Valery Hache/AFP/AFP via Getty Images.

Editor: Nicholas Croce; Designer: Matt Cauli; Photo Researcher: Marty Levick